EROTIC

MW01171700

EROTICALLY

ANOINTED

AUTHORS TERRENCE REED SR. AND ANGEL REED

EROTICALLY ANOINTED

Table of Content

EROTICALLY ANOINTED

ANOINTED

Anointed…To ceremonially confer divine or hole office upon a priest or monarch. Anointed means to be consecrated, set apart or dedicated unto the Lord. Smeared with oil for an intended purpose.

EROTICALLY ANOINTED

Whether you are a preacher, deacon, musician, or those God chooses to use at His will. You are anointed for a purpose. The anointing comes from God but doesn't separate us from our natural being. With all this great anointing God has bestowed upon us, we have not lost our natural affections. The anointing empowers us to do what we have been called to do in the Spirit, but our natural man is still controlled by human behavior. Holding hands, kissing or showing any gesture of affection is all-natural behavior. We have been programmed to view this behavior of those with an anointing as a bad thing, and that's not necessarily the case. We are multi-dimensional beings and can have more than one experience at a time. Being anointed does not take away our ability to be erotically aroused. In fact, when the anointing is high, our sexual arousal is heightened, and the physical man is in full beast mode. This arousal can only be satisfied by touch, taste, or smell......"May your breasts be like clusters of grapes on the vine, the fragrance of your breath like apples, and your mouth like the best wine. May the wine go straight to my beloved, flowing gently over lips and teeth". (Song of Solomon 7:8-9) Even Solomon and all his concubines, knew the effects of touch, taste and smell!

King David was considered a man after God's own heart; he also had an erotic side. In fact, his erotic desires were so great, old and bedridden, a young damsel was put in bed with him. When he didn't try to consume her, they thought the King was dead! Can you imagine having an appetite for sex so strong, not acting on those urges causes folk to think that you're dead?!

David housed both attributes. He was both erotic and anointed. The same holds true for us!! Let's explore this notion together and embrace being...

e-ROTICALLY a-NOINTED!

EROTICALLY ANOINTED

ANTICIPATION

Anticipation…To stand in expectation or excitement. To wait eagerly for something to happen. To look ahead to what's to come and believe with certainty it will happen.

EROTICALLY ANOINTED

MOST… not all Christian couples were taught they had to settle for a boring sex life. The topic of sex for years has been taboo in most churches and Christian homes. We have been taught that sex should not be talked about or mentioned in our sanctuaries. We have become so detached from reality where sex is concerned, that it has hurt, broken or damaged marriages. Sex is an extension, a plus, a bonus to marriage. A good sex life allows you to build and maintain a healthy marriage. It heightens the intimate part of marriage, where the two agreed to become one. You're able to accept any flaws or even quirks the other may have. The physical attraction remains long after the hype of a big wedding. The love between the two grows stronger. The bond intensifies.

EROTICALLY ANOINTED

Productive and meaningful communication is not an awkward or "hard conversation" to have.

God's purpose for intimacy between a husband and wife was always meant to be something beautiful. A connection in the spirit that would draw the two closer. A connection so powerful the two literally felt like they are one.

The frequency of sex in marriage may change after some time. That's no reason sex must become mundane or a forced activity. With all of life's happenings, whether it be work, finances, kids or even ministry, KEEP SEX A PRIORITY!!

Often time when sex or intimacy is mentioned in certain circles, church being the biggest one, it's usually in a derogatory form. We have been plagued

EROTICALLY ANOINTED

with scandals of infidelity and sexual immorality. Too often we hear about the negative aspects of sex and intimacy, until it starts to affect your mental. We can't do this, or we can't do that because of what someone may think.

Hebrews 13:4 of the Bible says, "Marriage is honorable in all, and the bed chamber is undefiled: This scripture tells us the bed chamber is pure! What happens in YOUR bedroom between a husband and wife is pure and good!

I believe it's time that we deal with the topic of sex in a positive light. Sex among the married can be enjoyed without the feeling of guilt.

EROTICALLY ANOINTED

Wholesome sex for the married couple should be exciting and breathtaking! Each encounter should be liberating and maximizing!

We are human beings, with human emotions and desires. God created us with these emotions and desires. We must learn there is nothing wrong with enjoying sex! We we're created to please our spouse! Why have we put limits on the act of pleasing our significant other? Think back on the times you literally put thought into acts of appreciation. When was the last time you put thought into acts of affection? The desire to please and be pleased on every level requires strategic planning, as you hold on to lingering anticipation. When these thoughts and actions are properly communicated to your spouse,

EROTICALLY ANOINTED

the desire and want for you increases the anticipation for Eroticism!

According to Webster…. Eroticism: A state of sexual arousal or anticipation from stimulation of erogenous zones! For some this could be a touch or a look. For others a thought and some a certain smell. Eroticism is ANTICIPATION!!!!

Eroticism is anticipation and anticipation means to look forward too. Husbands and wives should be eagerly awaiting the chance to come together. Build on those thoughts and acts throughout the day. Do something spontaneous or completely out of your norm! Send a "For Your Eyes Only" picture to your spouse. Some may say this is so childish or unnecessary, but did you smile when you read that suggestion? Were you turned on by the fact your spouse thought to send the picture? Were you erotically aroused? Folk post everything on social media. Send your spouse pics of what they have at home and watch the time they spend on social media go down. You get in your spouse DM! But that's a book for another time. If your comfort level is not there, share your favorite photo of the two of you. How about a "just because" call that has nothing to do with bills or kids or what's for dinner. You were simply thinking about them, and you pictured yourself kissing the stress of their day away. We're in the texting age..

> Hey my love! Dinner is prepared, wine is chilled, I'm wearing nothing but that string lingerie you like and heels! Hurry Home!!

EROTICALLY ANOINTED

You have not only reassured them of your love, but your commitment to your marriage and raised that erotic anticipation to levels that lead to baby making or at least The Act!!

We will always provide Biblical clarity. More so for those who cannot quite leave behind "learned behavior" from lack of or bad teaching.

1 Corinthians 7:5 says there's only one reason why you shouldn't be having sex. And even this has to be with mutual consent, so you can fast and pray. Even after that Paul says come together again SOON, so the devil doesn't tempt you. Even the devil knows you're supposed to have a healthy sexual relationship. He manipulates couples into thinking it's no big deal, but then sets up temptation in the form of just what

you like. If it wasn't a big deal or big part of marriage, why would he be trying to destroy it? Paul closes by saying come together again and often!

Your erotic anticipation should be so high that the enemy has no chance in infiltrating your union. Look forward to getting together every chance you get. Song of Solomon describes a man with adjectives like bolt, Lebanon cedar, and tree barks. The woman is described with just about every fruit known to man, soft and sweet. How erotic a sex session would be when you view your spouse with appealing adjectives. Build your anticipation by stimulating your thoughts and understand that pleasing your spouse is both purposeful and pleasurable!

EROTICALLY ANOINTED

Consider for a moment this story…Couples embrace your Erotic Anointing!!!

This morning seemed different, I'd been leaving for work at 5:30 am and getting home well into the late-night hour. As you can imagine, by the time I get home the house is quiet and wifey is already in bed. This was far from our norm; regular date nights and pillow talk time is more our speed. With the late workdays, quality time has been limited.

This particular Sunday morning, while I'm preparing to minister, I noticed my wife get out of bed wearing one of my t-shirts. This was way different from the silky items she normally chooses. There was nothing special about this shirt, no special design or saying printed on it. It was mine and she was wearing it!

EROTICALLY ANOINTED

This small act became a sexual trigger! Just her walking from the bed to the bathroom in my t-shirt turned me all the way on! I was so turned on; I couldn't focus on preparing my sermon. As I'm meditating for morning service, my mind kept wandering from the message to being obsessed with the thought of jumping her bones! The phrase "fill me up until I overflow" took on a whole different meaning and I had planned to do just that. I sat the iPad and laptop aside, left the Bible on the nightstand and followed her into the bathroom. The thirst was mutual, her body language said she wanted me just as much as I was wanting her. Without saying a word, we began kissing each other passionately. US time had been limited so the anticipation was crazy hot.

EROTICALLY ANOINTED

We both had a strong desire, strong want and strong need to feel the other.

Knowing we only had a few minutes before the start of our day and church, the intimacy became more intense, passion was high and body temperatures was rising! Then…..there was a knock on the door. Our son had awakened, still rubbing sleep from his eyes, he asked the question… What ya'll doing? Ugggghhh blocker! The one moment we've had in days, now interrupted! Something had to give. We needed quality time for grown up activities. We were both hot, horny and in need of a serious release, freely and as often as we wanted.

Making that happen had become my personal mission. I had to get us away. Yes, I'm anointed to preach the gospel, but I'm also a man with sexual

needs, wants and desires. I'm both erotic and

anointed, and at that moment… I was Erotically

Anointed! Wifey was about to get a date night she'd

think about for days.

EROTICALLY ANOINTED

ATTRACTION

Attraction… The action or power to evoke interest,

liking, pleasure or desire for something or someone.

that's emotional, romantic, sexual or physical. The

feeling of being attracted involves your physical

senses, your hormones and your nerves. Attraction

makes you want to go to a certain place or do a

particular thing.

EROTICALLY ANOINTED

The anointing was on me so heavy when we reached the church house, I preached a sermon titled God's about to give you that "One Good Thing"! Jeremiah 33:14; Behold the days come, saith the Lord, that I will perform that good thing which I have promised unto the house of Israel and to the house of Judah.

I had some one good thing promises of my own to instill upon my wife! After service, I decided to step my game up. The encoded conversation during the ride home was enticing. Hands entwined was suggestive foreplay of what was to come. Once home I put on my grey sweatpants along with a fitted "iShifted" t-shirt and began preparing dinner. I knew how much wifey loved when I cooked for her. She

EROTICALLY ANOINTED

gets weak when I wear my sweats… aka men's lingerie!

For me, it was full steam ahead. I had an agenda, and I would not be denied. My plan was definitely working. As I was cooking, she began texting me her favorite pictures of us. Pics of us on vacation, date nights, various events, and a few car selfies. I caught her snapping a picture of me while I was cooking and noticed she began to blush. I used the old trick; can you help me for a minute just to get her in the kitchen. Instead of giving her a task, I put my arms around her, kissed her forehead and massaged her shoulders. I ran my hands down her back and caressed her phatty as I whispered in her ear how

EROTICALLY ANOINTED

beautiful she was and let her feel the bulge in my sweatpants that said I want you.

Flirting is a sexual behavior that can be also used on a social level, involving body language, spoken and at times written communication. It signifies an attraction or interest and has been used as a gauge or indicator of what's to come. Relationally flirting should be fun, playful and exciting interaction between you and your spouse. Flirting can and will reinforce one's self-esteem. Flirt with your spouse often! Know their limits and what they are comfortable with and watch the response you receive. Flirting is just a continued gesture from courting and chasing after them. You are letting your mate know you are still into them. Sexual attraction seems to dwindle in marriages. Most times

it's because you have stopped flirting with each other!
Mix things up! Change your pattern and daily routine
and allow tension and expectation to build. Frequent
reassuring does wonders for a relationship!

What does your personal resume of your mate consist
of? Would you list a bunch of characteristics common
in a mate... provider, hard worker, handy, and/or
good helpmate? Or would your resume be more
personal and specific to qualities that give you
butterflies still such as... gentle touch, great kisser,
amazing lover, extremely affectionate, pleasure
pleaser, emotionally in tune with me! My person, my
mate, my love, my best friend! It's the couples that
have taking the time and put the work into "learning"

their mate intimately. These are the couples who are well versed in the others likes, dislikes, personality quirks, their goals and dreams are the couples who make it to "Happily Ever After"!

Cruising is "OUR" thing! We enjoy traveling the world. Embarking on new excursions and adventures. One being a little more adventurous than the other. (Insider). The point is we found something we both enjoy doing. We're free spirited and enjoy life on the high seas. When we plan a cruise, much thought goes into the various "activities" we will embark upon. Preparation is everything. We shop for each other. Buying whatever it is we want to see the other end. This gets risky! But we're married and our bed is undefiled!

EROTICALLY ANOINTED

Consider for a moment this next story…Couples embrace your Erotic Anointing!!!

It's embarkation day! We're filled with excitement and anticipation. Not only to be cruising, but also to enjoy every moment of these next four days without the norm of life… life-ing. We explore the ship as we always do, locating our usual ship activities. During one cruise wifey convinced me to take a Latin dance class knowing I can't dance. Once I put my Brooklyn two step to it, I actually enjoyed this experience. We grab a bite to eat and head to our cabin to change and start this cruise off right! The plan is to pick out the others outfit for the evening. The outfit she's wearing at the moment is looking good to me. I watch as she steps out onto the balcony to take in the sights of

EROTICALLY ANOINTED

Miami. SN: Christian couples!! It's OK to be saved, don't throw away your sexy!! All outfits do not have to be "church attire"! Men and women alike enjoy seeing their mate as eye candy. We are visual beings. Present yourself in a manner that will always spark an interest for your spouse. Sexy is not only in what you wear. Your attitude and body language plays a major role as well. Your demeanor and posture play an important part in setting the mood…. Unbeknown to her, watching her stand there, seeing the perfect curve of her apple bottom and how the denim shorts showed just enough cheek to give me an arousal. I walk out onto the balcony and began to massage her shoulders. Her response to my touch made her more attractive, than if she was wearing lingerie. She arched her back and leaned against me, she placed her hands on my face and ran her nails down my beard. At that moment she was enjoying her husband! Not the Bishop, not the Pastor her husband. This small gesture helped me relax and exhale. No rules, no limitations, and restrictions. Just like that, I was far away from the church and church folk with their opinions. Right now, I'm a husband about to fully partake in grown folk pleasures with my wife. Her next move took me completely by surprise. She's usually reserved and more of the respondent. She leads me inside and heads for the shower! The steam from the shower fills the cabin, the aroma of her perfume mixed with the hot water is giving off a sweet scent. The physical and emotional connection was undeniable. An unshakable bond was created, and any barriers had fallen away. The warmth of the water intensified intimacy as all stress and worries were washed away. The flow of the water induced a light hypnosis taking us to our "erotic place".

Water… whether it's a river, an ocean, or shower, evoke a vast array of a person's emotions. Water is a tranquil and calming element. Water assists in promoting feelings of balance and clarity. Sometimes, you just need to get to the water!

ARRANGEMENT

Arrangement…The action, process or result of

arranging or being arranged for a particular purpose

or activity. To make plans or preparations for a future

event. To put in order or prepare in advance.

EROTICALLY ANOINTED

This arrangement was about to go into full effect!

Imagine you're enjoying a bonfire; the flames are warm and inviting. In order to maintain the fire, new wood must continuously be added as a source of fuel. If this is not done, the flames will eventually die down until there's nothing left but smoke and ash. Apply this same analogy to marriage. With time you easily get caught up in daily mundane chores such as work, kids, ministry, and forget to add wood to your marital bonfire. NEVER STOP DATING!

Couples listen…. Stop feeling guilty for wanting to have a good time. There's no shame in taking time for adult play dates! As long as no unethical and immoral rules are broken, learn to enjoy yourself, your spouse and life again! Because of my anointing, I allowed the

opinions of church folk cause me to live in a box.
Coming out of that box freed me and allowed me to
minister on a greater level and lead by example. I'm
living this anointed life while enjoying doing life with
my spouse. No church titles… just Mr. and Mrs.

Date nights should be arranged and set to occur at
least once a month and take place at times….
OUTSIDE YOUR HOME! Arranged date nights
provide opportunities for different types of interaction
from everyday activities you already do together.
Many couples after being together for years,
experience a feeling of disconnect. Things that once
made you feel excited and important now seem
routine and mundane. The key is to date no matter the

circumstance. A walk in the park together, a picnic, or even a long drive with no particular destination.

The most important thing is consistency: Consistently show up for your spouse and show you care by adding wood to your martial bonfire! Keep the novelty alive in your marriage with intentional effort.

Consider for a moment this next story...Couples embrace your Erotic Anointing!!!

On the fly, I booked us at an Adults Only All-Inclusive Resort in Jamaica! Being travel agents I got a really good deal; she received the confirmation email and with a look of intrigue and hesitation inquired with me as to what I was up too! I stated we was trying something different, something outside the

EROTICALLY ANOINTED

box. Flying to our destination was much different than taking a cruise. Finding a spot in Jamaica was a task, I had to consider the culture, didn't want to embark upon anything vulgar or that would compromise our anointing or who we are. It's not a sin to travel and experience things outside of the church. This resort was amazing! Our bungalow was picturesque floating above turquoise waters. We stepped on to the ocean view glass floors in time to see a school of the most beautiful colored fish. There was also a soaking tub and private infinity pool, I was already having thoughts on ways to baptize our souls and come up speaking another language or two. This was going to be the perfect exotic experience. Time to relax and enjoy each other's company. As we stood out admiring how beautiful this island was, we saw a water taxi approaching. I took her hand and went inside; I needed us to prepare for my surprise.... Couples massage! She giggled the entire time with delight. Listen…. Happiness is the best way to get the BEST out of your spouse. There is nothing they won't make happen for you that will benefit the both of you! We've always talked about getting massage together, now we could place a checkmark next to it on our bucket list. We slid into matching swim wear. I hear my wife talking to someone or something named fupa, now I didn't want to mess up the moment, so I played along and started talking to fupa as well. Be good and stay flat fupa she said, so I jumped in the conversation and countered with fupa getting loved on tonight. Now with the look she threw my way, I know she purposely didn't point to it, look it's way or touch it just to see if I really knew what she was talking about. She must've forgot for a moment she was married to the Prophet! One look in her eyes and God himself told me who this fupa was! I smiled as I walked towards her and laid these anointed hands on fupa and declared you will stay flat! She let out the biggest laugh, and just like that the anointing saved our trip. Sometimes it's the smallest and simplest things that will creep in and change moods, atmospheres, attitudes, and marriages. You must stay in tune with each other, acknowledge the little things and address them together.

We emerge to lit candles and incense giving a sweet romantic aroma. Soft music was playing in the background as the friendliest and professional staff was setting up. Being our first couples massage I had to lay some ground rules on this masseur! Don't touch anything that's covered! We had plans to handle that part ourselves later that night. This was different, edgy but comfortable. We held hands as we felt the warmth of the oil hit our backs. We engaged in light conversation while giving each other "that eye" not knowing if what we were feeling was supposed to feel like that. Our every need was catered too, we were served wine and Jamaican patties. The couples massage turned out to be a great idea, definitely pillow talk conversation for later. The word erotic causes people to think of sexual acts only. When any intimate encounter brings on warm, fuzzy I love you always feelings it's an erotic moment! We explored a private yacht excursion which turned out to be one of the best highlights of our trip. Not only did we experience some of the most amazing views, she sweet talked me into getting on a jet ski which to my surprise I enjoyed! But I drew the line at snorkeling, I watched from the boat as wifey jumped into the clearest blue water. My wife swims extremely well, but we were in the middle of this open ocean and swimming to me means at any point my feet can still touch ground. As funny as that may sound, it's a word for somebody. At any point in your marriage make sure your feet are still touching ground, solid ground, a sure foundation. A foundation built on love, trust and communication.

They didn't exclude me, while she enjoyed snorkeling, I embarked on fishing, something I know

EROTICALLY ANOINTED

I can do. What happens when you get a man in his element? He talks trash! As much as I was talking, I was also praying, Lord let something grab hold of this hook. Now I don't know if any of this was preplanned, but dinner consisted of fresh caught red snapper and lobster. Candlelit dinner caught fresh and prepared in the middle of the ocean! Talk about an experience!

It was well into the evening when we arrived back at our bungalow, once inside I handed her a small box wrapped in black and topped with an orange bow and a card that read… put on what's inside and meet me in the private pool. I've been waiting a long time to see her in this getup. Those voluptuous curves were looking extremely good, leaving nothing to my

EROTICALLY ANOINTED

imagination. Absolutely gorgeous, beauty in living color. The moon's light reflecting off her body, the water glistening like crystals. The temperature of the pool has increased a few degrees, the movement of the water will carry us into the night... to our erotic place...

EROTICALLY ANOINTED

AROUSAL

Arousal… the state of being stimulated to a point of perception. To be in a state in which you feel excited or very alert. Arousal is your body's natural mechanism for accessing pleasure.

EROTICALLY ANOINTED

Arousal plays an important role in regulating consciousness, attention, decision making, learning and memory. It's a motivating factor for certain behaviors such as motor coordination, mobility, and sexual activity. There are several factors that can prevent a person from being aroused, I want to hound in on two I feel are most important in a marriage, boredom and self-esteem. Life is an adventure when shared with someone you love! There is an erotic anointing in everything we do. We learned to put down our phones and spend that time with each other. We love dancing together, laughing together whether it's something humorous or an awkward moment. We always reassure each other of being THAT person for life.

EROTICALLY ANOINTED

It's that arousal I get from knowing my person gets me, my person has my back, my person is cheering for me to win. Some of our best work is done outside the bedroom when we are aroused by each other. A smile from me takes away every care throughout her day. A kiss blown at me just before I preach, causes the heavens to open and I preach until His Glory falls. Share gratitude and appreciation and give credit where it's due. We have a saying… "It's the little things" that really matter the most. It's the little things we often reminisce on, it's the little things that shakes up our daily routine.

Consider for a moment this next story…Couples embrace your Erotic Anointing!!!

EROTICALLY ANOINTED

We were having the time of our lives; she knew she was stimulating my senses. Every look, the way she moved, laying on the hammock, intentionally posing on the beach. Must have been the high humidity of the day or the strong rays of the sun but every gesture was bringing on a strong arousal. The way she looked at me with those seductive eyes, blowing kisses with those luscious lips and giving me sexual innuendos. Could have been the signs that only I was getting that caused an even greater arousal. She was laying it on thick, giggling in between each act of wifely conduct! So, this is what she wanted to do today…. Being erotic as I am, I decided two can play that game. I eased up behind her, put my arms around her and began to pull her close, face to neck. The feel of my beard always turns her on. I move around as if I was

EROTICALLY ANOINTED

going to give her a kiss but instead pulled my phone out and took a selfie! Her face turned beet red, I couldn't tell if she was blushing or in shock! But I got the reaction I was looking for and raised the bar for this game of cat and mouse she started.

Many couples for some reason or another, have frowned or shied away from public displays of affection. Some can't even explain why or give the famous answer "this is just how we are". I'm totally against lewd acts in front of people. But a kiss, a hug, holding hands, rubbing a leg under the table at a restaurant or even a love tap across the butt is acceptable behavior for married couples. It shows the world you are in love with one another, and you don't mind expressing that love openly. Arousal is a prerequisite to foreplay. Once the mind has been stimulated, everything else comes naturally. When there's regular displays of affection, it doesn't take much to arouse your mate. Once your mate believes you enjoy them as much as they enjoy you, the littlest thing will turn them on. You notice the smell of new perfume or cologne. A fresh haircut, new hairstyle, or in my wife's case a new hair color will have you role playing without knowing it! We often times feel like newlyweds, each of us looking for ways to make the first move. Being intentional with arousing the other, which in turn makes our love sessions more erotic and intense. Be honest with yourself, coming off a long and stressful day of work and/or ministry, an erotically filled and intense love session is just what you need! OK… this next statement will ruffle some

feathers…. It's ok to be a little "NASTY"!! There, I
said it…Nasty! I can hear folk talking now. The
Bishop shouldn't be talking about being nasty. And
why not?! Ministry is a part of who we are and what
we do, and with all we put into ministry, the same
energy, love and excitement has to be put into
maintaining a healthy and happy marriage. Yes, the
Bishop sends his wife text messages asking what do
you have on? First lady recognizes the sign and falls
right into role. "In his shade I sat down with great
delight, And his fruit was sweet and delicious to my
taste". (Song of Solomon 2:3) Now if the young
Shulamite woman can taste of Solomons sweet
nectar, why would you limit the acts of your spouse?!

EROTICALLY ANOINTED

You cannot be so closed minded and brainwashed that you push your spouse away and the two are "just existing". That's not living! Come out of yourself… literally and arouse that man! Arouse that woman and allow your erotic anointing to take your marriage to the next level.

EROTICALLY ANOINTED

Assume The Position

Assume the position means to take over the role and responsibilities of a particular job or act. To turn away, with one's hands in a visible and unmovable position.

EROTICALLY ANOINTED

Keep it interesting…. It's important to keep it spicy in the bedroom. Move away from the same positions, the same time, the same foreplay moves. There is absolutely nothing wrong with changing the where, when and positions. Spontaneous encounters are always fun. Break all the rules and let that bad boy or bad girl loose. Do something totally unexpected. Be honest… You've been thinking… if I had the opportunity I would…. Or if I had the chance I would…or I would just love too…... Apply these same what ifs to your marriage! Go ahead and create some of these "what if moments"! Be aggressive and do what you've always wanted to do or try! When two people agree to commit to each other for the rest of their lives, it provides a level of security as well as other wonderful perks of being married. With growth,

EROTICALLY ANOINTED

and ever changing wants and desires this security can start to feel stale or boring. When love becomes more of an "attachment" it ceases to be fulfilling. Don't allow your marriage to fall into the "never have I ever" category. Create moments that you will remember for a lifetime. This is when you need a jump start from the predictability that has become your norm and assume the position! Go beyond the normal I love you and say something that will completely catch your spouse off guard. My love for you is a soul connection where there is no visible seam, thank you for being my happily ever after. Thank you for making me feel as if I am your everything, doing life with you is one of my greatest treasures. This is a welcomed reassurance that will have your spouse ready to assume the position.

EROTICALLY ANOINTED

Cherish the friendship and life long best friend you have in your spouse. You can never take them, their love, nor the life they share with you for granted. Only a lifelong commitment provides security for passion, creativity, and vulnerability of great sex!

I was never one to gossip, my wife taught me that pillow talk is not gossiping. This is our time to converse about our day, things we don't agree with and reiterate our goals and desires. Pillow talk can lead to some of the best sex sessions. Picture laying in bed talking and your spouse slides their hand down your thigh and gently caresses your manhood! This gesture will quickly make you forget what you were saying and quickly arouse every erotic fiber of your being!

EROTICALLY ANOINTED

Who else better to have those what if, would have, could have, should have experiences with other than your spouse! Join your spouse in the shower, share the warmth of the water and wash the stress of each other's day away. On the staircase! In the laundry room! During COVID our backyard became our private oasis! Our adult playground. We setup a camping tent with an inflatable mattress and created an instant Netflix and chill moment! Your spouse is whom you should be fulfilling all of your fantasies and desires with. Be comfortable enough to explore your spouse. It's moments like these that offer the perfect opportunity to perform all of those tricks you've been fantasizing about. Who would have thought this setup would afford us the opportunity to try some new adventures and revisit some oldies but

EROTICALLY ANOINTED

goodies. "Your stature is like that of the palm, and your breasts like clusters of fruit. I will climb the palm tree; I will take hold of its fruit". May your wine go straight to my beloved, flowing gently over lips and teeth!(Song of Solomon 7:7-9) With that.... The Sunset shadowing sixes and nine's is one of the most erotic scenes you can imagine. Changing scenery and positions can give your sessions a whole new experience. It enhances the moment and shifts the mood quickly. It creates an atmosphere for erotic pleasure with the simple change of fragrance or unexpected touch. It's satisfying and fulfilling, knowing we're both being pleased and pleasured. High energy, high vibration love making, high vibration sex, sometimes it's good to lay hands suddenly and assume the position...

AWAKENED

Awakened…Rouse, to bring out of sleep or caused to feel excited. To be made aware of a person's direct metaphysical connection.

EROTICALLY ANOINTED

An erotic awakening is a shift from subconsciousness to reality of all those thoughts you only allowed to live in your mind. Moving past your thoughts and awakening your body to experience something greater than your imagination. Feed off your spouses love language, know what awakens them. In doing so you will notice an increased level of closeness and desire from your spouse. Awakening your inner most desires and fantasies, is like having that lightbulb over your head finally light up and you have an "I Get It moment"! You realize behind every hard emotion displayed by your spouse, a soft emotion is masked. You finally get that a question asked several times is covering feelings of vulnerability. And behind that giggle is their alter ego provoking you into a bang session your spouse enjoys but would never normally verbalize. Our trips, our vacations, our "US time triggered an awakening in us that allowed our marriage to catapult to higher levels. We realized there was a wholesomeness to our sensuality. This eroticism was genuine and pure. There is nothing dirty or negative associated with our newfound sexual freedom. We had connected with emotions that had been suppressed for far too long. This type of affection for my spouse was natural and Biblical. Sex was created for spiritual as well as natural satisfaction. Songs of Solomon 4:16 bears witness to this. "Blow on my garden, that its fragrance may spread everywhere. Let my beloved come into his garden and taste its choice fruits".

EROTICALLY ANOINTED

Embracing our erotic anointing not only brought on greater sexual gratification but we found we did more than just love each other; we are actually IN LOVE with each other.

Never again will we let the false narratives about sex and sensuality dictate how we live our lives. Most issues in a marriage can be resolved with honest conversations and a healthy sexual relationship and being open minded. A lot of what we were taught was just wrong, so we believed wrong. This bad teaching not only affected black marriages, but black churches and the black community as a whole. We must unlearn and relearn as well as teach the truth. We have been programmed that something as sacred as sex, affection, unconditional love was disgusting, taboo and not needed. My wife and I are on a mission to teach the truth! Healthy sex is good for healthy marriages! Let's break the stigma surrounding sex and happy and healthy marriages. Especially the church circles and black culture. How about doing that for the culture! It's possible to be an anointed vessel and a sensual being, DemReeds live this every day. One does not take away from the other, in actuality it enhances. It does not mean we're acting in a carnal state, we are human and have learned some needs are not requiring spiritual intervention but the erotic and sensual touch from your spouse. We are spiritual beings having a natural experience.

e-ROTICALLY a-NOINTED!!!

EROTICALLY ANOINTED

We thank you all for your support. We hope something was said to rekindle the bonfire in your marriage. We pray stronger martial bonds and unconditional love that will spread throughout your family and communities. Let's change the narrative on love, sex and marriage.

Embrace Your EROTIC ANOINTING!!!

WWW.ISHIFTED.COM

#DEMREEDS

EROTICALLY ANOINTED

ACKNOWLEDGEMENT

We are truly thankful to all our family and friends that provided their valuable time and guidance. We stand humbled at the amount of love, support and understanding received as we embarked on this much needed project. His Bonnie Her Clyde truly describes our bond! The way we have loved and encouraged each other. Pushing and motivating each other in sharing just a piece of our story. The long nights and early mornings were definitely worth it. A big thank you to our children, Erica, Terrence Jr, Zaynah, Jazmine and Treydon. Our grandchildren Jaliyah, Zamir, Jayla, Jenesis, Harmony, Wynter and Harlem.

Made in the USA
Columbia, SC
03 March 2025

54659953R00035